THIS PLANNER BELONGS TO:

_____

dear you,

Welcome to another year of everyday chances to become your brightest self! In your hands is a daily planner, yes, but also a companion and guide to help you see and embrace who you already are and invite you to become more of who you wish to be! For years, I spent way too much time regretting the past or fretting about the future until a beloved friend pulled me aside. "You're missing your one beautiful life," she said, gently. "All you have is right now." Yes. This truth was the encouragement I needed to refocus on the present, the moment-by-moment opportunity we all have to grow and discover what is and what's possible. My hope is that this journal, divided into twelve aspirational themes, will encourage you to ponder and play, appreciate and aspire, cultivate and connect—and to see that every day is truly a chance to begin with you.

love, Marianne

be intentional

An **INTENTION** is a purposeful path to becoming your bravest, brightest self—in *all* areas of your life! As you look ahead to the next twelve months, use this space to jot down your biggest hopes and visions.

What you want to **DO**. Who you want to **BE**.
What you wish to **ATTRACT**. How you want to **FEEL**.

Have fun and dream big.
Every day is a new beginning.

my intentions

MONTH:

to-do:

SUNDAY	MONDAY	TUESDAY

WEDNESDAY	THURSDAY	FRIDAY	SATURDAY

monthly goals

WHAT WORKED LAST MONTH & MY PROUDEST MOMENT

WHAT COULD BE BETTER

NEW GOALS TO FOCUS ON

INSPIRED ACTIONS TO TAKE

be present

PRESENCE is the open-hearted embrace of the here and now, a moment-by-moment invitation to accept reality, honor your journey, see the beauty, find the lessons, welcome possibility, and choose what makes your soul come alive. It's meeting each moment, no matter what it holds, and knowing you have what you need.

Close your eyes and take a breath.
That's it. You're here, you're present.
Be you and begin anew.

Living with presence is noticing the now. Complete the lines below to create your own presence poem.

I feel _____

I know _____

I see _____

I hear _____

I sense _____

I am _____

the week of _____

to-do:

MON	
TUE	
WED	
THU	
FRI	
SAT	
SUN	

hopes & intentions for the week:

Take a breath break. Put your right hand on your heart and cover it with your left, close your eyes, and take a deep breath. Repeat the words:

"I am here" on the inhale,

and *"I trust my life"* on the exhale.

Repeat for five breaths. How do you feel?

the week of _____

to-do:

	MON

	TUE

	WED

	THU

	FRI

	SAT

	SUN

hopes & intentions for the week:

Beginner's mind is seeing something with an open mind and fresh eyes, to notice details and opportunity, cultivate wonder and possibility. It changes the way you move about in the world.

Choose an object and write down details you haven't noticed before.

the week of _____

	MON

	TUE

	WED

	THU

	FRI

	SAT

	SUN

to-do:

hopes & intentions for the week:

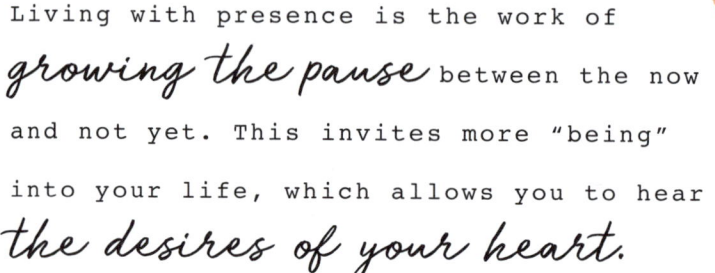

Living with presence is the work of *growing the pause* between the now and not yet. This invites more "being" into your life, which allows you to hear *the desires of your heart.*

Name three desires you have:

the week of _____

	MON

	TUE

	WED

	THU

	FRI

	SAT

	SUN

to-do:

hopes & intentions for the week:

MONTH:

to-do:

SUNDAY	MONDAY	TUESDAY

WEDNESDAY	THURSDAY	FRIDAY	SATURDAY

monthly goals

WHAT WORKED LAST MONTH & MY PROUDEST MOMENT

WHAT COULD BE BETTER

NEW GOALS TO FOCUS ON

INSPIRED ACTIONS TO TAKE

LOVE is a feeling and behavior toward others and yourself. It is affection and unconditional acceptance. Kindness, patience, compassion, and forgiveness, too.

Love wishes and inspires.

Heals and hopes.

Love is sacrificial and selfless.

Easy and tremendously hard.

Love takes practice and is contagious.

More love is always good.

Write a person's name to whom you wish to send loving energy. They can reside close to you or live far away. Focus inward. *Imagine love as a radiant light inside you.* Breathe deeply into your heart and picture this beloved person. *Send rays of love-filled energy outward,* envisioning your person receiving them.

If you could say anything to them from the heart, *what would you say?*

the week of _____

to-do:

☐ **MON**

☐ **TUE**

☐ **WED**

☐ **THU**

☐ **FRI**

hopes & intentions for the week:

☐ **SAT**

☐ **SUN**

What is the most *loving thing* you can tell yourself today?

the week of _____

MON	
TUE	
WED	
THU	
FRI	
SAT	
SUN	

to-do:

hopes & intentions for the week:

Think about the people you're closest to. What do you love about them? What qualities do you have that you think they *love about you?*

the week of _____

to-do:

MON

TUE

WED

THU

FRI

hopes & intentions for the week:

SAT

SUN

Loving yourself means letting go of past mistakes.

Think of something that makes you feel bad, embarrassed, or ashamed.

What do you need to forgive yourself for?

Write it down, close your eyes, then scribble it out and release regret from your body. Draw a heart below it when you've completed this practice.

the week of _____

- [ ] **MON**
- [ ] **TUE**
- [ ] **WED**
- [ ] **THU**
- [ ] **FRI**
- [ ] **SAT**
- [ ] **SUN**

to-do:

hopes & intentions for the week:

MONTH:

to-do:

SUNDAY	MONDAY	TUESDAY

WEDNESDAY	THURSDAY	FRIDAY	SATURDAY

monthly goals

WHAT WORKED LAST MONTH & MY PROUDEST MOMENT

WHAT COULD BE BETTER

NEW GOALS TO FOCUS ON

INSPIRED ACTIONS TO TAKE

be creative

CREATIVITY is your soul made visible. You are a unique expression of life, and creativity is the medium to get what's inside of you...out.

Creativity is the simple process of bringing something new into being in the way only you can, whether making, writing, speaking, observing, experimenting, gardening, cooking, problem-solving, knitting, doodling—whatever sparks freedom and energy within you!

Creativity is the calling card of your one-of-a-kind humanness.

What creative pursuits did you love as a child?

Are there any you'd want to try again now? Reconnecting with past delights often informs a continuing of creative self-expression.

the week of _____

MON

TUE

WED

THU

FRI

SAT

SUN

to-do:

hopes & intentions for the week:

Creativity needs new inspiration.

How can you mix up your routine in tiny ways? Take a new route to work, bike instead of walk, or listen to a different kind of music.

What will you try this week?

the week of _____

- [ ] **MON**

- [ ] **TUE**

- [ ] **WED**

- [ ] **THU**

- [ ] **FRI**

- [ ] **SAT**

- [ ] **SUN**

to-do:

hopes & intentions for the week:

Give yourself permission.

Often, we talk ourselves out of something before we try, believing we won't be successful. **Think of one thing you'd love to try, then fill in the blanks:**

I give myself permission to be a beginner at

_____

_____

_____

I release _____

_____

_____

the week of _____

MON

TUE

WED

THU

FRI

SAT

SUN

to-do:

hopes & intentions for the week:

"I am not creative."

How does this lie stand in your way? **Think about what your creativity actually looks like, and describe it in the space below.**

Example:

My creativity is expressed in unique and personal ways.

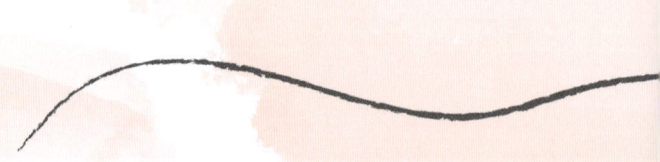

the week of _____

□ **MON**

□ **TUE**

□ **WED**

□ **THU**

□ **FRI**

□ **SAT**

□ **SUN**

to-do:

hopes & intentions for the week:

Give your mind and body some breathing room. Wander a book, art, gardening, or home improvement store and see what topics draw your attention. Take a hike or bike ride. *Leave the phone at home and let your inner voice whisper new desires.*

What interesting topics found you this week?

the week of _____

- [ ] **MON**

- [ ] **TUE**

- [ ] **WED**

- [ ] **THU**

- [ ] **FRI**

- [ ] **SAT**

- [ ] **SUN**

to-do:

hopes & intentions for the week:

MONTH:

to-do:

SUNDAY	MONDAY	TUESDAY

WEDNESDAY	THURSDAY	FRIDAY	SATURDAY

monthly goals

WHAT WORKED LAST MONTH & MY PROUDEST MOMENT

WHAT COULD BE BETTER

NEW GOALS TO FOCUS ON

INSPIRED ACTIONS TO TAKE

be playful

PLAYFULNESS is lighthearted, silly, and joy-sharing. Levity and laughter. When was the last time you did something just for fun without outcome, productivity, or judgment attached? Somewhere on our way from kid to grown-up, play and expansiveness is traded for work and schedules. Busyness and commitment admonish frivolity.

Look at your life and see the playground awaiting you.

It's time to recommit to light-heartedness!

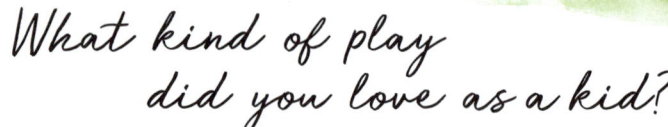

What kind of play did you love as a kid?

Think about the grown-up version. Climbing trees? Consider indoor rock climbing. Play-Doh or coloring? Maybe add a pottery or watercolor class to your schedule. **What will you try?**

the week of _____

MON

TUE

WED

THU

FRI

SAT

SUN

to-do:

hopes & intentions for the week:

List a few things that make you laugh out loud. *Who brings silliness to your life?* **Write their names below.** Are they in your life right now? If you can, perhaps reach out with a text or call.

the week of _____

MON

TUE

WED

THU

FRI

SAT

SUN

to-do:

hopes & intentions for the week:

At what age did you feel like your most fun self?

What were you doing then? **What's changed?**

the week of _____

□ MON

□ TUE

□ WED

□ THU

□ FRI

□ SAT

□ SUN

to-do:

hopes & intentions for the week:

What does play mean to you?

PLAY IS THE SOUND OF

PLAY IS THE TASTE OF

PLAY IS THE SMELL OF

PLAY IS THE FEELING OF

the week of _____

MON	
TUE	
WED	
THU	
FRI	
SAT	
SUN	

to-do:

hopes & intentions for the week:

MONTH:

to-do:

SUNDAY	MONDAY	TUESDAY

WEDNESDAY	THURSDAY	FRIDAY	SATURDAY

monthly goals

WHAT WORKED LAST MONTH & MY PROUDEST MOMENT

WHAT COULD BE BETTER

NEW GOALS TO FOCUS ON

INSPIRED ACTIONS TO TAKE

be well

WELLNESS is the tending and keeping of extraordinary you—your body, mind, and spirit. Wellness is strength and peace, aliveness, vitality, and connectedness.

Wellness is wholeness.

And seeking help to get there if and when needed. Wellness is the practice and pursuit of healthy habits that allow you to thrive versus survive.

You are the only you, unrepeatable.

Wellness is choosing to nurture your true self with the exquisite care and intention you deserve to live your happiest, healthiest life.

What is one thing you can do this week to tend to your *physical wellness?*

the week of _____

to-do:

| MON |
| TUE |
| WED |
| THU |
| FRI |
| SAT |
| SUN |

hopes & intentions for the week:

Write several uplifting affirmations here that can encourage your wellness.

I accept myself.

I am inviting goodness into my life.

the week of _____

☐ **MON**

☐ **TUE**

☐ **WED**

☐ **THU**

☐ **FRI**

☐ **SAT**

☐ **SUN**

to-do:

hopes & intentions for the week:

What things
bring you peace
when you are feeling stressed or anxious?

the week of _____

- MON
- TUE
- WED
- THU
- FRI
- SAT
- SUN

to-do:

hopes & intentions for the week:

Designate a sacred space for yourself to think or simply be. A favorite chair or walking trail. A yoga mat or meditation cushion.

What is this space for you?

Carve out time this week for stillness in this place.

the week of _____

to-do:

MON

TUE

WED

THU

FRI

hopes & intentions for the week:

SAT

SUN

MONTH:

to-do:

SUNDAY	MONDAY	TUESDAY

WEDNESDAY	THURSDAY	FRIDAY	SATURDAY

monthly goals

WHAT WORKED LAST MONTH & MY PROUDEST MOMENT

WHAT COULD BE BETTER

NEW GOALS TO FOCUS ON

INSPIRED ACTIONS TO TAKE

be generous

GENEROSITY is a mindset and way of being toward others and yourself.

You have enough.

There is enough.

More is not better.

There is plenty to share with others.

Generosity is knowing and trusting that when you open your hand and heart to give, you are blessed in ways you cannot imagine. A generous heart overflows with contentment and appreciation for what already is. Generosity is an act of love, and it makes a difference.

Write down three ways you can
be generous this week.

the week of _____

MON

TUE

WED

THU

FRI

SAT

SUN

to-do:

hopes & intentions for the week:

What is a charity or passion that is close to your heart?
Is there a way to offer your time or resources in a new way?

the week of _____

MON

TUE

WED

THU

FRI

SAT

SUN

to-do:

hopes & intentions for the week:

How do you need help?

That's right. Is there someone whose generosity you would like to benefit from, be it advice or time? Perhaps it's a colleague, neighbor, or friend.
Write their name and what you need below.

the week of _____

MON

TUE

WED

THU

FRI

SAT

SUN

to-do:

hopes & intentions for the week:

Name a time you were the recipient of generosity.

What was it, and how did it make you feel?

the week of _____

to-do:

- [ ] **MON**

- [ ] **TUE**

- [ ] **WED**

- [ ] **THU**

- [ ] **FRI**

hopes & intentions for the week:

- [ ] **SAT**

- [ ] **SUN**

List three ways you have *abundance* in your life right now.

the week of _____

to-do:

- MON
- TUE
- WED
- THU
- FRI

hopes & intentions for the week:

- SAT
- SUN

MONTH:

to-do:

SUNDAY	MONDAY	TUESDAY

WEDNESDAY	THURSDAY	FRIDAY	SATURDAY

monthly goals

WHAT WORKED LAST MONTH & MY PROUDEST MOMENT

WHAT COULD BE BETTER

NEW GOALS TO FOCUS ON

INSPIRED ACTIONS TO TAKE

be connected

CONNECTION is the act of paying attention to yourself and being open and available to others. Heeding the whispers of your own heart and leaning into the voices of others.

Connection is listening and learning, empathy and compassion, commitment, honesty, and acceptance.

Connection is being seen and known, a co-traveler on life's road. Connection is feeling cared for and a sense of belonging.

Connection is essential to our aliveness, sense of purpose, and well-being.

To connect with others, you need to first connect with yourself. Check in with yourself.
How are you feeling this week?
Do you need to act on any of these feelings?

the week of _____

to-do:

MON

TUE

WED

THU

FRI

hopes & intentions for the week:

SAT

SUN

What and who are the
five most sacred connections
in your life right now?

the week of _____

MON

TUE

WED

THU

FRI

SAT

SUN

to-do:

hopes & intentions for the week:

Is there someone or something *you're being called to connect with right now* even if you aren't quite sure why?

the week of _____

MON	
TUE	
WED	
THU	
FRI	
SAT	
SUN	

to-do:

hopes & intentions for the week:

Create a "connection corner" in your living room, bedroom, or office by assembling a few items—for example, a photograph, candle, or special rock—that remind you of your relationship to yourself and others. What items did you choose, and why are they meaningful to you?

the week of _____

to-do:

- MON
- TUE
- WED
- THU
- FRI
- SAT
- SUN

hopes & intentions for the week:

You can connect to yourself through solitude.
What is a favorite activity you enjoy alone?

the week of _____

☐ MON

☐ TUE

☐ WED

☐ THU

☐ FRI

☐ SAT

☐ SUN

to-do:

hopes & intentions for the week:

MONTH:

to-do:

SUNDAY	MONDAY	TUESDAY

WEDNESDAY	THURSDAY	FRIDAY	SATURDAY

monthly goals

WHAT WORKED LAST MONTH & MY PROUDEST MOMENT

WHAT COULD BE BETTER

NEW GOALS TO FOCUS ON

INSPIRED ACTIONS TO TAKE

be kind

KINDNESS is *a way of being* in life. You've heard the familiar quote:

Be kind, for everyone is fighting a hard battle.

Giving kindness is simple and free. Friendly, generous, considerate, and helpful. It's patient and understanding. Kindness is sometimes easy, often hard, and *always* good for the soul.

What is a *random act of kindness* you can do this week for someone else?

the week of _____

- [ ] **MON**

- [ ] **TUE**

- [ ] **WED**

- [ ] **THU**

- [ ] **FRI**

- [ ] **SAT**

- [ ] **SUN**

to-do:

hopes & intentions for the week:

Recall a time when
your kindness changed someone's mood, day, or life.

the week of _____

MON

TUE

WED

THU

FRI

SAT

SUN

to-do:

hopes & intentions for the week:

Think about a time you were on the *receiving end of kindness.* What was it and how did it make you feel?

the week of _____

	MON

| | TUE |

| | WED |

| | THU |

| | FRI |

| | SAT |

| | SUN |

to-do:

hopes & intentions for the week:

I can be *kinder to myself* by

the week of _____

MON

TUE

WED

THU

FRI

SAT

SUN

to-do:

hopes & intentions for the week:

MONTH:

to-do:

SUNDAY	MONDAY	TUESDAY

WEDNESDAY	THURSDAY	FRIDAY	SATURDAY

monthly goals

WHAT WORKED LAST MONTH & MY PROUDEST MOMENT

WHAT COULD BE BETTER

NEW GOALS TO FOCUS ON

INSPIRED ACTIONS TO TAKE

be adventurous

ADVENTURE is living with an open heart, embracing your life with a courageous willingness to consider different ideas, try new things, contemplate the impossible, face your fears, and seize opportunity. Life is a journey, not a destination.

Adventure is tiny and tremendous, quiet and loud, close to home and far away.

Feeling that adventurous spirit, you say? Try a new thing. Take the risk. Face a fear. Make memories. Say yes and expand yourself.

What is one thing you can say yes to this week to break out of your comfort zone and stoke your adventurous spirit? *Start small.*

the week of _____

- [ ] **MON**
- [ ] **TUE**
- [ ] **WED**
- [ ] **THU**
- [ ] **FRI**
- [ ] **SAT**
- [ ] **SUN**

to-do:

hopes & intentions for the week:

Create an *adventure bucket list*
with some things you'd like to try and do.

the week of _____

MON	
TUE	
WED	
THU	
FRI	
SAT	
SUN	

to-do:

hopes & intentions for the week:

What is one of your most
memorable adventures?
What did you learn about yourself through it?

the week of _____

to-do:

☐ MON

☐ TUE

☐ WED

☐ THU

☐ FRI

hopes & intentions for the week:

☐ SAT

☐ SUN

Find a photo that reflects your most adventurous self. What were you doing? *What do you admire about that person?* Is there anything you can learn from them now?

the week of _____

- [ ] **MON**
- [ ] **TUE**
- [ ] **WED**
- [ ] **THU**
- [ ] **FRI**
- [ ] **SAT**
- [ ] **SUN**

to-do:

hopes & intentions for the week:

What are three *limiting beliefs* you carry inside that stop you from trying new things?

the week of _____

MON

TUE

WED

THU

FRI

SAT

SUN

to-do:

hopes & intentions for the week:

MONTH:

to-do:

SUNDAY	MONDAY	TUESDAY

WEDNESDAY	THURSDAY	FRIDAY	SATURDAY

monthly goals

WHAT WORKED LAST MONTH & MY PROUDEST MOMENT

WHAT COULD BE BETTER

NEW GOALS TO FOCUS ON

INSPIRED ACTIONS TO TAKE

be wise

WISDOM is the knowledge you've gained through living your life. And it's often your hardest seasons that teach you the most about your strength and resourcefulness.

To be wise is to listen more, talk less. Understand more, judge less.

Put things in perspective before you jump to conclusions. Wisdom is the great pause that allows you to choose what you deeply know versus what's quick or popular. Wisdom is curious and open-minded, thoughtful and calm, hard won and heart-centered.

Who have been some of your "*wisdom mentors*" in your life?

the week of _____

MON

TUE

WED

THU

FRI

SAT

SUN

to-do:

hopes & intentions for the week:

One of the biggest ways we gain wisdom is *by making mistakes.* What is one of the biggest lessons you've learned this year? What about ever?

the week of _____

MON

TUE

WED

THU

FRI

SAT

SUN

to-do:

hopes & intentions for the week:

Wisdom can come from unexpected places.

Have a conversation this week with someone you don't know or someone you don't speak to very often, like an elderly neighbor or a child. **Jot down a few things from that interaction that you can learn from.**

the week of _____

MON

TUE

WED

THU

FRI

SAT

SUN

to-do:

hopes & intentions for the week:

Jot down some *new experiences* that could *expand your perspective.* Make a visit to a museum, new city, or part of town. Read a memoir or biography. **Choose one to do this week and write your choice below.**

the week of _____

to-do:

| MON |
| TUE |
| WED |
| THU |
| FRI |
| SAT |
| SUN |

hopes & intentions for the week:

MONTH:

to-do:

SUNDAY	MONDAY	TUESDAY

WEDNESDAY	THURSDAY	FRIDAY	SATURDAY

monthly goals

WHAT WORKED LAST MONTH & MY PROUDEST MOMENT

WHAT COULD BE BETTER

NEW GOALS TO FOCUS ON

INSPIRED ACTIONS TO TAKE

be grateful

To cultivate **GRATITUDE** is to look for the good—despite the hard.

Gratitude is a choice,

a way of seeing the world that lets you find beauty in the ordinary, bright spots in struggle, miracles in the mess, and purpose in the pain.

Gratitude is cultivating a spirit of appreciation

that makes what you already have more than enough. It is the path to a peaceful, contented, happy, and spacious life.

What is your own definition of *gratitude?*

the week of _____

- [ ] **MON**

- [ ] **TUE**

- [ ] **WED**

- [ ] **THU**

- [ ] **FRI**

- [ ] **SAT**

- [ ] **SUN**

to-do:

hopes & intentions for the week:

Write about one way you are
choosing gratitude right now
in light of something difficult.

the week of _____

to-do:

☐ **MON**

☐ **TUE**

☐ **WED**

☐ **THU**

☐ **FRI**

hopes & intentions for the week:

☐ **SAT**

☐ **SUN**

Write about ordinary beauty.

What parts of your everyday can you grow deeper gratitude for?

the week of _____

MON

TUE

WED

THU

FRI

SAT

SUN

to-do:

hopes & intentions for the week:

Share a gesture of gratitude with someone special to you.

Send a text or note of appreciation or give a compliment. **What will you say?**

the week of _____

MON

TUE

WED

THU

FRI

SAT

SUN

to-do:

hopes & intentions for the week:

MONTH:

to-do:

SUNDAY	MONDAY	TUESDAY

WEDNESDAY	THURSDAY	FRIDAY	SATURDAY

monthly goals

WHAT WORKED LAST MONTH & MY PROUDEST MOMENT

WHAT COULD BE BETTER

NEW GOALS TO FOCUS ON

INSPIRED ACTIONS TO TAKE

be celebratory

CELEBRATION is pausing to acknowledge, applaud, or rejoice. It's an opportunity to celebrate yourself or someone else for achieving, persevering, succeeding, being.

Celebration doesn't have to recognize just the big stuff like birthdays, graduations, or promotions. It can honor everyday living as well. First steps, last chemo, the arrival of a season, the finishing of a project, the full moon, last day of school, or first snowfall.

It's celebrating another day gifted and every sacred breath filling it.

Write three things you can celebrate

about your own humanness, like your patience, adventurous spirit, or sense of humor.

the week of _____

☐ **MON**

☐ **TUE**

☐ **WED**

☐ **THU**

☐ **FRI**

☐ **SAT**

☐ **SUN**

to-do:

hopes & intentions for the week:

Is there someone in your life who can use some acknowledgment? *How can you share your appreciation of them today?*

the week of _____

to-do:

| MON |
| TUE |
| WED |
| THU |
| FRI |
| SAT |
| SUN |

hopes & intentions for the week:

To savor means to enjoy.
What can you savor this week?

the week of _____

MON

TUE

WED

THU

FRI

SAT

SUN

to-do:

hopes & intentions for the week:

Looking back over the past twelve months, write down a few things *you wish to celebrate.*

the week of _____

- MON
- TUE
- WED
- THU
- FRI
- SAT
- SUN

to-do:

hopes & intentions for the week:

names & addresses

Name _____
Address _____
City _____ State _____ Zip _____
Phone _____
Email _____

Name _____
Address _____
City _____ State _____ Zip _____
Phone _____
Email _____

Name _____
Address _____
City _____ State _____ Zip _____
Phone _____
Email _____

Name _____
Address _____
City _____ State _____ Zip _____
Phone _____
Email _____

Name _____
Address _____
City _____ State _____ Zip _____
Phone _____
Email _____

Name _____
Address _____
City _____ State _____ Zip _____
Phone _____
Email _____

Name _____
Address _____
City _____ State _____ Zip _____
Phone _____
Email _____

Name _____
Address _____
City _____ State _____ Zip _____
Phone _____
Email _____

Name _____
Address _____
City _____ State _____ Zip _____
Phone _____
Email _____

special occasions & birthdays

notes

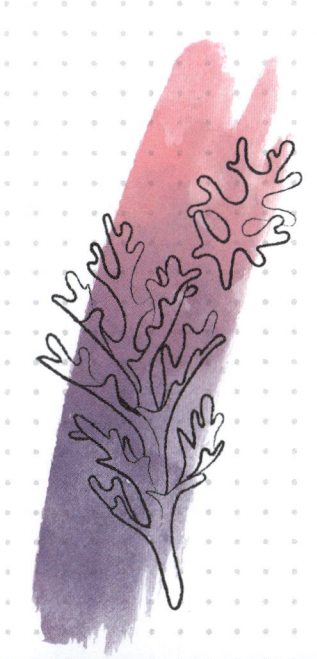

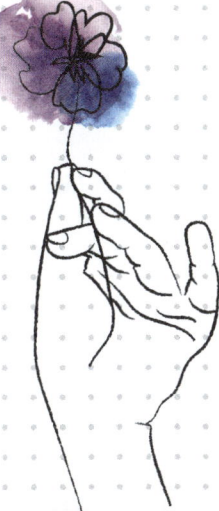

Copyright © 2022 by Marianne Richmond
Cover and internal design © 2022 by Sourcebooks
Cover and internal design by Danielle McNaughton/Sourcebooks
Cover images © coolvector/Freepik; Artnizu/Shutterstock;
Liliana Danila/Shutterstock
Internal illustrations on pages 48, 49 © Marianne Richmond
Internal images © Freepik, Shutterstock

Sourcebooks and the colophon are registered trademarks of Sourcebooks.

All rights reserved. No part of this planner may be reproduced in any form or by any electronic or mechanical means including information storage and retrieval systems—except in the case of brief quotations embodied in critical articles or reviews—without permission in writing from its publisher, Sourcebooks.

All trademarks and copyrights are acknowledged as being the properties of their respective owners and no sponsorship, affiliation, or endorsement is claimed or implied.

Published by Sourcebooks.
P.O. Box 4410, Naperville, Illinois 60567-4410
(630) 961-3900
sourcebooks.com

Printed and bound in China.
OGP 10 9 8 7 6 5 4 3 2 1

appointment	appointment	appointment	appointment	appointment
appointment	appointment	appointment	appointment	appointment
appointment	appointment	appointment	appointment	appointment
appointment	appointment	appointment	appointment	appointment
appointment	appointment	appointment	appointment	appointment
plans	plans	plans	plans	plans
plans	plans	plans	plans	plans
plans	plans	plans	plans	plans
plans	plans	plans	plans	plans
plans	plans	plans	plans	plans
celebrate!	celebrate!	celebrate!	celebrate!	celebrate!
celebrate!	celebrate!	celebrate!	celebrate!	celebrate!
celebrate!	celebrate!	celebrate!	celebrate!	celebrate!
celebrate!	celebrate!	celebrate!	celebrate!	celebrate!
celebrate!	celebrate!	celebrate!	celebrate!	celebrate!
birthday	birthday	birthday	birthday	birthday
birthday	birthday	birthday	birthday	birthday
birthday	birthday	birthday	birthday	birthday
birthday	birthday	birthday	birthday	birthday
birthday	birthday	birthday	birthday	birthday
a day off	a day off	a day off	a day off	a day off
a day off	a day off	a day off	a day off	a day off
vacation!	vacation!	vacation!	vacation!	vacation!
grateful	grateful	grateful	grateful	grateful
play day!	play day!	play day!	play day!	play day!
me time	me time	me time	me time	me time

important!	important!	important!	important!	important!
important!	important!	important!	important!	important!
important!	important!	important!	important!	important!
important!	important!	important!	important!	important!
important!	important!	important!	important!	important!
don't forget	don't forget	don't forget	don't forget	don't forget
don't forget	don't forget	don't forget	don't forget	don't forget
don't forget	don't forget	don't forget	don't forget	don't forget
note to self:	note to self:	note to self:	note to self:	note to self:
note to self:	note to self:	note to self:	note to self:	note to self:
note to self:	note to self:	note to self:	note to self:	note to self:
meeting	meeting	meeting	meeting	meeting
meeting	meeting	meeting	meeting	meeting
meeting	meeting	meeting	meeting	meeting
meeting	meeting	meeting	meeting	meeting
meeting	meeting	meeting	meeting	meeting
GOALS	GOALS	GOALS	GOALS	GOALS
GOALS	GOALS	GOALS	GOALS	GOALS
GOALS	GOALS	GOALS	GOALS	GOALS
to-do:	to-do:	to-do:	to-do:	to-do:
to-do:	to-do:	to-do:	to-do:	to-do:
refresh	refresh	refresh	refresh	refresh
reset	reset	reset	reset	reset
self-care	self-care	self-care	self-care	self-care
me time	me time	me time	me time	me time
fresh start	fresh start	fresh start	fresh start	fresh start